# The Book of Nuggets

**Chicago EOS Implementers®**

Copyright © 2024 by Dan Heuertz, Dan Wallace, Dan Zawacki, Paul Detlefs, Tania Bengtsson, Beth Fahey, Deb Venable, Bobi Siembieda, Charlton Keultjes, Kevin Hundal, Rene' Boer, Steven Solano, Eric Larsen, John McMahon, and Clark Neuhoff

All rights reserved.

No portion of this book may be reproduced in any form without written permission from the publisher or authors, except as permitted by U.S. copyright law.

EOS®, The Entrepreneurial Operating System®, and EOS Implementer® are all registered trademarks owned by EOS Worldwide, LLC. For a complete list of trademarks owned by EOS Worldwide throughout this book/e-book, please visit branding.eosworldwide.com/eos-trademarks/.

This book is not intended to teach EOS®. To learn about EOS®, please visit https://eosworldwide.com. This book is published with the support of EOS Worldwide to share nuggets of wisdom developed through experiences as EOS Implementers.

This publication is designed to provide accurate and authoritative information in regard to the subject matter covered. It is sold with the understanding that neither the authors nor the publisher are engaged in rendering legal, investment, accounting or other professional services. While the publisher and authors have used their best efforts in preparing this book, they make no representations or warranties with respect to the accuracy or completeness of the contents of this book and specifically disclaim any implied warranties of merchantability or fitness for a particular purpose. No warranty may be created or extended by sales representatives or written sales materials. The advice and strategies contained herein may not be suitable for your situation. You should consult with a professional when appropriate. In no event shall the publisher, the authors, EOS Worldwide or any other party be liable for any loss of profit or any other commercial damages, including but not limited to special, incidental, consequential, personal, or other damages, as a result of your use of any methods described in this book.

ISBN: 979-8-9899876-1-0 (Paperback)
ISBN: 979-8-9899876-5-8 (Digital)
Book Cover by 100covers.com
Edited by Ben Heuertz
1st Edition 2024

The Skinny Platform is a place for entrepreneurs with something to share and want to be heard. These Skinny Books are how we say it.

Skinnies help entrepreneurs establish authority and intellectual property without writing just another business book no one will read. By working through our process entrepreneurs can go from an idea to a book in 90 days at less than half the cost of comparable services. Finally, we help entrepreneurs break through all the noise of the business book world by writing short, digestible, valuable books and sharing them with our audience.

What makes a Skinny so unique and valuable are our core values:

1. Brevity - Written to be read in under an hour
2. Collaboration - True partnership with our authors
3. Experience Share - Vulnerable & Relatable Stories
4. Framework - Learn & Grow with our books
5. Be Heard - Break through the noise as an author & thought leader

For more information visit theskinnyplatform.com or contact us at info@theskinnyplatform.com

# Contents

Foreword .................................................................................... 1

Appreciations ............................................................................. 3

Gratitude Made Simple ............................................................... 4

Rules of Engagement.................................................................. 6

Creating A Plan For Rock Completion ....................................... 8

The Emotional Link: Connecting Purpose to Long-Term Goals ............ 10

Updating Your Structure............................................................ 12

Lead with Love .......................................................................... 14

The Greater Good Of The Organization................................... 16

Voice Of The Customer............................................................. 18

Proud, Not Perfect..................................................................... 20

The Power of Prioritization: Making Time for What Matters ................ 22

The Hiring Process.................................................................... 24

Tackling People Challenges..................................................... 26

Change the People or Change the People.............................. 28

Connecting Human Energy o n e n e s s................................. 30

Win the Week............................................................................. 32

# Foreword

The genesis of this little book dates to 2008. I transitioned from having been a business owner to becoming a business coach within an organization created by my friend, Gino Wickman. I was teaching, coaching and facilitating meetings with owners and leadership teams of entrepreneurial companies helping them clarify, simplify and realize their vision. I gained a deeper appreciation for the courage it takes to start a business, and the discipline it takes to build that business.

By 2011, there were a handful of us teaching the same time-tested, simple tools and process to help business owners in Chicagoland get more of what they wanted from their business. We were "friendly competitors", but I realized we could be so much more if we focused on being "healthy collaborators". With that in mind, we met for the first time to share insights and tips. We quickly realized that by having an abundance and help-first mindset we could be better together and provide greater value for our clients.

Over the years, we met each quarter to share something we called "Nuggets" – little pearls of wisdom served up by our members that they had gleaned from facilitating sessions with their clients. A Nugget is something small, simple, easy to digest, that delivers big value. The Nuggets in this book are contributed by 15 exceptional members of our Chicago collaborative meeting who've helped over 800 entrepreneurial companies become their best.

I am very fortunate and grateful to have played a part in building this wonderful team of people who share the same values and have a passion for helping others be the best they can be. I believe that life is a series of fortunate accidents made all the better by the people you help and the people that help you.

My good friend, Dan Heuertz, created the concept for this "Skinny Book" to accomplish two things:

1. Create an abundance and help-first mindset
2. Contribute to a worthy cause

*The Book of Nuggets*

100% of the royalty from this book will go directly to Freedom Reads (See QR code below). I hope you will find this book helpful and that you'll share it with others.

Be your best and do your best,

Rene' Boer

# Appreciations

We want to share a huge thank you and appreciation with the collaborators that participated in this book. Thank you to:

John McMahon

Rene' Boer

Dan Zawacki

Paul Detlefs

Eric Larsen

Dan Wallace

Steven Solano

Kevin Hundal

Deb Venable

Tania Bengtsson

Dan Heuertz

Charlton Keultjes

Beth Fahey

Clark Neuhoff

Bobi Siembieda

# Gratitude Made Simple

### By Steven Solano

Gratitude is a powerful force that can significantly impact personal and professional life. As someone who discovered the transformative power of gratitude later in life, I can attest to its ability to turn one's life around. This nugget of wisdom focuses on making gratitude a simple, actionable practice in our daily lives.

In my 20s, I approached life trying to "get" something for myself. As I matured, I realized that giving sincerely from the heart had much better results. This shift from a scarcity mindset to an abundance mindset has consistently led to positive outcomes.

Research supports the benefits of gratitude. Studies have shown that practicing gratitude can improve mental and physical health.

There are 5 steps I use to make gratitude simple.

1. **Commit to Daily Gratitude Action**: Move beyond mental appreciation to actively expressing gratitude to others. This could be as simple as telling someone how grateful you are for them or creating a positive experience for someone.

2. **Research the Benefits of Gratitude**: Educate yourself on the factual benefits of gratitude. A wealth of information is available, including studies and health-focused content.

3. **Set Your Daily Gratitude Hour**: Establish a specific time each day for gratitude reflection. For me, it's the hour before sunset. Use this time to pause and reflect on your day, efforts, and attitude.

4. **Get Creative in Expressing Gratitude**: There are no rules for expressing gratitude. It doesn't require monetary investment, just your heart, and good intentions.

5. **Surround Yourself with Grateful People**: Choose to associate with individuals with a grateful heart and an abundance mindset. This may mean letting go of relationships that don't align with this philosophy to make room for more positive influences in your life.

Your gratitude practice doesn't need to be time-consuming. Even a few seconds of mindful appreciation during your designated gratitude hour can be impactful.

Remember, a gratitude practice is similar to building muscle, requiring consistent effort. Through anchoring your practice to a daily occurrence, like the sunset, you create a sustainable habit.

In a business context, surrounding yourself with individuals who have an abundance mindset and a grateful heart can be energizing and productive. These interactions tend to be more positive and balanced compared to those with individuals focused solely on personal gain.

By cultivating gratitude in your personal life and your business practices, you can create a more positive, energetic, and impactful professional environment. This approach not only benefits you personally, but can also lead to greater success and satisfaction in your entrepreneurial endeavors.

Remember, gratitude is a simple yet powerful tool that costs nothing but can yield significant returns in all aspects of life.

# Rules of Engagement

### By Rene' Boer

One of the most common challenges for a leader is to improve accountability within their team. A powerful solution is to establish simple "Rules of Engagement" - a set of agreed-upon behaviors that team members commit to upholding. Once established, the rules provide the framework for peer-to-peer accountability.

To be effective with this approach, the leader must be:

- Humble
- A role model
- Willing to be held accountable by their team

**Follow these four steps:**

1. Gather the team and ask: "Could we agree on a few simple rules that we can live by to make our team more effective?"
2. Encourage them to suggest behavioral rules that might include the following:
   - Being on time for meetings
   - Honoring commitments
   - Turning off mobile phones
   - No blaming or shaming
   - No excuses
   - Listening to understand
   - Speaking up
3. Narrow the list to four or five key rules and ask each person: "Are you willing to live by these rules?" Ensure each person agrees.
4. Discuss how the team will handle a situation where any member (including the leader) violates the rules.

**This leads to:**

1. **Shared Responsibility**: The leader no longer bears the sole responsibility for upholding the rules.
2. **Improved Discipline**: Members follow through and honor commitments.
3. **Enhanced Communication**: Members avoid making assumptions.
4. **Smoother Onboarding**: New members quickly learn that the "rules" are non-negotiable and that they will be held accountable by their teammates.

When rules are broken, they are addressed immediately by correcting the behavior without blaming, shaming, or making excuses. This reduces unnecessary drama and quickly reinforces the importance of the rules.

Following the rules of engagement can improve team health, clarity around expectations, and the overall effectiveness of the team.

# Creating A Plan For Rock Completion

### By Paul Detlefs

In EOS® there are 90-day priorities that are called "Rocks". These are crucial for building a better future for your business. These are typically projects that are important but not urgent, falling into Stephen Covey's quadrant of high importance and low urgency. The challenge lies in consistently completing these goals amidst the daily pressures of running a business.

Rocks are not just topics or vague ideas. They are specific, measurable priorities that are either completed or not - there's no middle ground.

The cornerstone of successful rock completion is having a detailed plan for each rock. The plans should be created within 1-2 weeks after your quarterly meeting and include:

1. **Clear Definition of "Done"**: Precisely describe what completion looks like.
2. **Importance and Impact**: Articulate why this rock is crucial and its potential impact on the business.
3. **Potential Obstacles**: Identify challenges you might face.
4. **Resource Requirements**: List the resources, including people, you'll need to complete the rock.
5. **Milestones**: Break down the rock into 3-5 key steps with associated deadlines.

**Next are the key Strategies to include in your plan:**

1. **Share Your Plan**: Inform all stakeholders, including team members and external parties, about your Rock and how they might be involved.
2. **Schedule a Rock Review**: Plan a longer rock review in your weekly meeting to present your plan and get feedback from teammates.
3. **Mid-Quarter Check-in**: Schedule a dedicated meeting halfway through the quarter to honestly assess progress.

4. **Embrace Healthy Conflict**: Encourage rock owners to be vulnerable about challenges, and team members to ask probing questions about progress.
5. **Calendar Blocking**: Schedule dedicated "rock time", treating it with the same importance as external meetings.
6. **Early Presentation**: Present your rock to the leadership team before the due date, even if it's not fully completed.
7. **Designate a Rock Captain**: Consider assigning a team member to oversee all rocks for the quarter, ensuring everyone follows best practices.

Remember, the value isn't in the plan itself, but in the planning process. Things may not go exactly as planned, but the act of thinking through your approach is invaluable. Coupled with peer-to-peer accountability in weekly meetings, this planning process can dramatically improve your rock completion rate.

By implementing these strategies, you can transform your approach to quarterly priorities. As one client demonstrated, consistently applying these principles can lead to rock completion rates of 95-100% over multiple quarters. The key is not just knowing these strategies but putting them into practice.

# The Emotional Link: Connecting Purpose to Long-Term Goals

### By John McMahon

Through my experience as an EOS Implementer®, I've discovered a powerful concept: the emotional connection between an organization's core focus and its long-term target. This connection can powerfully drive success and employee engagement.

**The core focus consists of two parts:**

1. The organization's purpose or passion - "The Why"
2. Its Niche - "The What"

When these elements are clear they can be translated into a tangible, ambitious goal measuring human impact. This becomes the long-term goal or as referred to with EOS®, the "Core Target".

The key insight is this: When we connect people emotionally to something larger than themselves, it becomes much easier to live, and lean on that passion. The long-term goal then becomes something that everyone can feel and sense in their own way.

For example, if an organization's passion is "helping people help other people," this might translate into a goal of "helping 100 million people by [future date]." This goal is:

- Larger than life
- Requires organizational growth and change
- Connects employees emotionally to the work

While quantifying the goal can make it more measurable, the precision of the number is often less important than the meaning and idea it's grounded in. The goal should be ambitious enough that the organization can grow, add capabilities, and step outside its current capabilities to achieve it.

We often approach business with a rational, logical view. However, while information and data can inform people about where we're going and what we're doing, emotion is what _moves_ people and inspires action. The emotional connection to why we're here can be the "secret sauce" that motivates people through tough days.

Uncovering an organization's true purpose and translating it into a long-term goal can take time. It requires vulnerability and authenticity from leadership. As a facilitator, I've found that encouraging storytelling can be a powerful tool. Asking clients to share stories about times their organization had a big impact can bypass mental filters and tap into genuine emotion.

In my practice, my purpose is "to inspire individuals and teams to reach beyond what they think they're capable of." My long-term goal is to impact 75 companies before I finish my career as an EOS Implementer®.

While setting and achieving goals is important, it's crucial to remember that the journey itself holds significant value. As we approach our targets, we should be prepared to set new ones or find fulfillment in the process itself.

By fostering this emotional connection, between purpose and long-term goals, organizations can create a more engaged, motivated workforce and achieve remarkable results.

# Updating Your Structure

### By Eric Larsen

The structure of an organization is often referred to as "the root of all good and evil in an organization." Defining your structure should go beyond traditional organizational charts and align with a strategy for growth. However, many teams become complacent after initial implementation.

The structure serves as the foundation of your organization. It defines who reports to whom and what each role is accountable for. With EOS®, the tool used to do this is the Accountability Chart®. As your business changes, your structure must change with it. Failing to update your structure can lead to misalignment, inefficient resource allocation, unclear roles and responsibilities, stunted growth, and scalability issues.

**Some signs that you need to revisit your structure are:**

1. Your company has hit a growth ceiling
2. You've entered new markets or business areas
3. Industry changes have altered how you operate
4. Attempts to delegate or streamline processes are failing

**When updating your structure, adopt this mindset:**

1. Imagine you're on the board of directors, starting the company from scratch. Ask, "What would the right structure look like if we start over?"
2. Focus on the greater good of the organization, not individual roles
3. Be prepared for potential changes in the leadership team
4. Have clear definitions for major roles without getting caught up in titles as titles convey ego.
5. Outline 5 major roles for each seat
6. One Person, One Seat: Enough said.

Consider this example: A manufacturer struggled with one person occupying sales and operations roles. Revising the structure and hiring a dedicated sales leader, significantly improved sales performance and operational efficiency.

**4 ways to maintain the structure include:**

1. Review the chart quarterly
2. Update it before new people join the organization
3. Ensure it aligns with your company's current goals and market realities. Is the accountability chart going to support the business goals for the next 2 to 4 quarters?
4. Conduct regular "spot checks" to verify its accuracy and relevance

Remember, your organization's structure is alive. It should evolve as your business grows and changes. Regularly revisiting and refining this tool ensures your organizational structure remains a catalyst for growth, rather than a constraint.

Embracing change in your structure is essential for scaling your business. It's often said, "What got you here might not get you to the next level." So be willing to make changes for the greater good of your organization, and you'll create a structure that supports success.

# Lead with Love

### By Deb Venable

From a young age, I was taught a valuable lesson by my mother: "Always be nice and never compare crosses." She explained that everyone carries burdens, and what may seem light to you could be very heavy for them. This has shaped my approach to both personal relationships and business leadership.

As an EOS Implementer®, I help entrepreneurs maximize their businesses' potential and create environments for healthy growth. Research shows that when people feel free to express themselves and are surrounded by tenderness and care it often leads to more satisfaction, stronger commitment, and higher accountability.

I have 3 simple ways I lead with love:

### 1. Embrace Vulnerability and Imperfection

I enter all relationships acknowledging my own vulnerability and imperfections. By dropping my guard, I show others that it's okay not to be okay or to not have all the answers. This approach encourages teams to come together more strongly, challenge the status quo, and brainstorm new opportunities with energy.

### 2. Stay Curious

Maintaining curiosity is crucial. Ask deep, pointed questions that encourage people to open up. Inquire about the 'why' behind decisions, statements, or actions. This open-mindedness often reveals important information that might otherwise remain hidden, allowing for more empathetic and effective leadership.

### 3. Suspend Judgment

It's not our place to judge others' priorities or goals. Every client and team member has a unique set of circumstances. Our job as leaders and facilitators is to love them and draw out their best contributions, embracing each person's unique qualities.

An essential component of leading with love is showing gratitude. Regardless of how challenging a day or session might be, I remain grateful for the opportunity to do what I love and work with phenomenal teams. This attitude of gratitude fosters a positive environment and continual growth.

Leading with love doesn't mean creating a weak, excuse-filled environment. Instead, it's about fostering a safe space where people can openly express their challenges, limitations, and needs. This approach allows for strong accountability while maintaining a supportive atmosphere.

This principle of leading with love extends beyond the business world. In personal relationships, including family dynamics, leading with love provides a way to navigate tough conversations. It's about approaching every interaction from a place of non-judgment, vulnerability, and curiosity, allowing the work to naturally follow.

Leading with love isn't being soft or avoiding hard conversations. When we lead with love, we create an environment where people feel safe to express themselves, take risks, and perform at their best. This approach not only enhances business outcomes but also enriches our personal lives and relationships.

# The Greater Good Of The Organization

### By Dan Zawacki

GGOTO, or the Greater Good of the Organization, is a principle that is crucial for companies aiming to align their teams and make effective decisions.

Many teams tend to focus on individual or departmental interests rather than the organization as a whole. This perspective can lead to silos being created within the company.

To combat this narrow focus, it's essential to elevate your perspective. Visualize this concept by drawing an arrow pointing to the top of your head, symbolizing the need to work "on" the business rather than "in" it. This 40,000-foot view allows you to make decisions that benefit the entire organization.

**You can use 4 easy tricks to implement GGOTO:**

1. **Visual Reminder**: Write "GGOTO" on the whiteboard during meetings as a constant reminder of this principle.

2. **Equal Voices**: Emphasize that everyone in the session room is equal, regardless of their position in the company. This equality encourages open disagreement and discussion for the benefit of the organization.

3. **Challenging Silos**: When creating the structure, be vigilant about avoiding the creation of departmental silos. Encourage cross-functional collaboration.

4. **Same Language**: Establish a unified vocabulary within the organization to enhance clarity and alignment.

Consider this example: Two co-owners who had a strained relationship were building two separate companies within one organization. By applying the GGOTO principle, we reconstructed their structure to reflect a single, unified company structure. This not only brought clarity to their employees but also improved the co-owners' working relationship.

*Chicago EOS Implementers®*

Through my experience as an EOS Implementer®, one of the lessons I have learned is that people in an organization do not have the ability to "read the label from outside the jar." This external viewpoint, and other implementers, allows for the identification of inefficiencies and misalignments that may not be invisible to those within the organization.

Remember, repetition is key. The concept of GGOTO needs to be consistently reinforced. As the saying goes, "You need to hear something seven times before you hear it the first time." Make GGOTO a part of your regular discussions and decision-making processes.

By consistently applying the GGOTO principle, teams can achieve stronger alignment, make better decisions, and ultimately become quicker, more efficient, and more profitable. It's a simple yet powerful concept that, when fully embraced, can transform an organization's culture and performance.

# Voice Of The Customer

### By Clark Neuhoff

While many things get loaded into a marketing strategy, the two most critical elements are simply—who we should talk to and what we should say—are crucial. These elements identify your ideal target market and unique value propositions. While this may seem oversimplified; it truly captures the essence of effective marketing.

When brainstorming what sets a company apart, leadership teams often focus on "table stakes" like good quality, competitive pricing, and punctuality. However, these are expected attributes that don't truly differentiate a business. To uncover genuine uniqueness, we must look deeper and, more importantly, listen to our customers.

I recommend conducting a "Voice of the Customer" exercise to understand what makes your company unique. This simple tool can provide invaluable insights into your company's value proposition. Here's how to conduct it:

1. Identify your best clients—those who have been loyal customers for years.
2. Request 20-30 minutes of their time, emphasizing that this is not a sales call but a request for feedback.
   - Consider having various team members conduct these calls, including those who don't typically interact with customers. This can provide fresh perspectives and deepen the organization's customer understanding.
3. Ask them a simple question: "You have choices in the marketplace, yet you've been buying from us for quite a while. Why us? Why do you keep coming back?"
4. Listen and record everything. After each response, ask, "Is there anything else?" until you get 3 reasons.
5. If time allows, ask two additional questions:
   - "Is there anything else you wish we could do for you that we're not doing?"
   - "Is there anything we do that you wish we would stop doing?"

6. Repeat this process with 10-20 customers.
7. Categorize the responses. You should see patterns emerge that either validate your perceived unique value propositions or reveal new ones that are even more compelling.

**After conducting the exercise:**
1. Follow up with customers on any suggestions or concerns they raised, even if you can't implement them. This shows respect and builds stronger relationships.
2. Use the insights to refine your marketing strategy and messaging.

One of my coaches would say, "Customers are dying to tell you what they want. They're dying for somebody to listen to what their problem is. You just got to ask." This exercise is about listening, not telling. It doesn't matter what you think makes you unique and special—what matters is what's in the customer's mind.

Conducting this Voice of the Customer exercise can uncover your true value propositions, strengthen customer relationships, and refine your marketing to resonate with your target audience.

# Proud, Not Perfect

### By Dan Heuertz

During the writing of my Skinny™ Book "Noisy Head," I discovered a powerful concept that I believe can benefit entrepreneurs and leaders: "Proud, Not Perfect." This simple phrase encapsulates a necessary mindset shift that can dramatically improve team dynamics and organizational progress.

As a visionary entrepreneur, I've witnessed firsthand the chaos that perfectionism can create. The pursuit of perfection often leads to:

- Added unnecessary complexity in decision-making
- Killed momentum
- Diminished team confidence

Consider this scenario: requesting a simple word change in a document. What seems like a minor adjustment can cascade into a series of time-consuming revisions, affecting the entire project's timeline and team morale.

Instead of striving for perfection, focus on being proud of your work. This approach:

- Encourages progress over stagnation
- Maintains forward momentum
- Builds confidence within your team

Remember, perfection is the enemy of progress. As leaders, our primary role is to build confidence and facilitate action.

To put "Proud, Not Perfect" into practice, consider adopting the 80% Approach From Strategic Coach by Dan Sullivan:

1. Complete your work to 80% of your best ability
2. Hand it off to a team member who can bring it to their 80%
3. If necessary, pass it to a third person for final refinement

**This collaborative method fosters:**

- More efficient progress
- Increased pride in collective work
- Higher confidence levels

**The other component to being proud of your work is understanding your work preferences:**

- Identify your optimal work durations & time of day (e.g., 30-60-90 minute sprints)
- Acknowledge when you need a co-creator
- Recognize when you've reached your 80% limit and need to hand off the work

By embracing the "Proud, Not Perfect" mindset, you can create a more dynamic, confident, and productive team environment. Remember, it's about the best work we can do together, not achieving an impossible standard of perfection.

# The Power of Prioritization: Making Time for What Matters

### By Charlton Keultjes

In my experience as an EOS Implementer®, I often encounter organizations hesitant to commit to quarterly off-site planning days. The common refrain is, "We're too busy to take a full day off every quarter." My response to this concern is: "You're not so busy that you can't spend a day offsite doing planning. You're so busy because you don't do a full day offsite every quarter."

Many businesses find themselves caught in a cycle of constant activity without clear direction:

1. Juggling a thousand tasks simultaneously
2. Making minimal progress on multiple fronts
3. Feeling stuck on a "hamster wheel" of busyness

This scenario stems from a lack of prioritization. When everything is important, nothing truly is.

**Quarterly off-site planning sessions offer several key benefits:**

1. **Prioritization**: Teams agree on the most critical tasks, focusing energy where it matters most.
2. **Alignment**: Ensuring all team members are moving in the same direction, rather than zigzagging toward goals.
3. **Efficiency**: By concentrating on fewer, more important tasks, teams actually create more time in their day-to-day operations.

**Committing to these planning sessions can be challenging:**

- It requires honest, sometimes difficult conversations about priorities.
- Team members must have the courage to question each other's focus areas.
- It demands transparency and a healthy team dynamic.

However, the payoff is substantial. As one client noted, "It's really nice knowing that we're on the same page." This alignment reduces the mental load on leaders and makes it easier to empower team members.

Imagine trying to get from point A to point B. Without prioritization: Team members move in different directions, creating a zigzag path that delays goal achievement. With prioritization: The team moves in a straight line, reaching objectives more quickly and efficiently.

The key takeaway is this: You won't know what's truly important unless you take the time to step back and assess. The discussions that happen during these off-site days often cover crucial topics that never arise in weekly meetings.

By investing time in prioritization and alignment, you create more time and focus in your day-to-day operations. It's not about working harder, but working smarter and more cohesively as a team.

Remember, being busy doesn't always equate to being productive. True progress comes from focused effort on the right priorities – and that begins with taking the time to identify what those priorities should be.

# The Hiring Process

### By Bobi Siembieda

Many organizations struggle with hiring the right candidates, often resulting in costly turnover and frustration. The solution to this challenge lies not in blaming recruiters or candidates, but in developing a comprehensive hiring process that goes beyond traditional job descriptions.

To understand a candidate's fit for a role, we must consider the 3 parts of the mind:

1. **Affective**: This relates to motivation, personality, and values. It's the driving force behind communication and purpose.
2. **Conative**: This represents instinctual behaviors and actions under stress, best measured by tools like the Kolbe A Index.
3. **Cognitive**: This encompasses skills, experience, and education – the traditional focus of most hiring processes.

**Developing a comprehensive hiring process:**

1. **Define the Role Thoroughly**: Go beyond a basic job description. Consider the values, motivations, and instinctual behaviors required for success in the role.
2. **Create Targeted Interview Questions**: Develop situational and behavioral questions that assess alignment with company values and role requirements.
3. **Utilize Multiple Assessments**: Incorporate tools like DISC, Predictive Index, StrengthsFinder, and Kolbe assessments to gain a holistic view of candidates.
4. **Implement Skills Tests**: Depending on the role, include relevant skills tests to objectively evaluate cognitive abilities.
5. **Standardize the Interview Process**: Create a rubric for interviewers to ensure consistent evaluation across candidates.
6. **Collaborative Decision-Making**: Bring interviewers together to discuss candidates, using the rubric as a guide

7. **Patience in Selection**: Resist the urge to hire quickly to fill a position. Don't hire to satisfy a rock; hire to hire the right candidate and just keep going until you find that right candidate.

Pay particular attention to the conative fit, as measured by tools like the Kolbe A Index. If the person's not wired to do it over time, their performance will degrade. They will be in a bad situation and so will you.

Once you've developed this comprehensive hiring process for a role, document it as part of your core processes. This allows for easier refinement and consistent application in future hiring rounds.

By implementing this thorough approach, organizations can significantly improve their hiring success rate, reducing turnover and enhancing team performance.

# Tackling People Challenges

### By Beth Fahey

One recurring problem I see most often in leadership sessions is getting people into the right roles. In EOS® we call this "Right People, Right Seat". This comes up because leaders tend to shy away from addressing it head-on.

**Why? Two main reasons:**

1. **Fear of conflict** – Nobody enjoys having those tough performance conversations.

2. **Fear of consequences** – What if addressing the issue means losing the employee and taking on their workload?

This hesitation often results in leaders sugarcoating feedback, which dilutes the message and prolongs the problem.

Humans are naturally wired to avoid pain, and while this instinct is normal, it can lead to significant challenges—especially for managers. We hesitate to address tough issues because we don't want to hurt feelings or make others feel judged. Managers often carry guilt for not addressing problems sooner, blaming themselves for the situations they're now in. They rationalize delays with excuses like, *"This isn't the right quarter,"* or, *"We just need to get through this ERP installation."*

Adding to the complexity, we bring our own baggage—personal narratives, emotions, and even "bad boss PTSD"—into conversations with our team members. We question our perceptions, doubting whether we're seeing things clearly, and slowly realize that we might be part of the problem. The fear of being wrong or exposing insecurities about our leadership role compounds the hesitation.

While we often know what we *should* do, delaying action feels easier in the moment. That's why I emphasize to my clients the importance of setting a self-imposed "expiration date" on people issues. This strategy prevents the trap of endless excuses and helps leaders take timely, constructive action.

Here's a simple rule: **One quarter to identify, one quarter to solve.** This gives you time to clarify the issue while ensuring timely action.

Generally, it takes about a quarter to discern if you're dealing with a people issue. To help determine whether you have a people issue, you can use an EOS® tool called The People Analyzer®. The People Analyzer® will help determine whether you have:

- **A Core Values Mismatch** – The person doesn't align with your company's values.
- **GWC® Issues (Get it, Want it, Capacity)** – The person lacks in one or more of these areas for their role.

Once identified, address the issue within the next quarter. Communicate this clearly when discussing "what's working" and "what's not working."

**To tackle these challenges effectively:**

- Be direct and to the point.
- Use your tools: scorecard measurables, rocks, and meeting participation as data.
- Frame your quarterly discussions around core values, rocks, and roles.
- Focus on what's working and what isn't.

As my mentor René Boer wisely says, *"When you keep someone in a seat where they don't belong, you're essentially stealing their life."* Holding someone in the wrong role not only limits their potential but also denies them the opportunity to find a place where they can truly thrive. It keeps them from becoming the best version of themselves—even if that means succeeding at another company.

By embracing this principle and applying the "one quarter to identify, one quarter to solve" approach, you can tackle people issues effectively. This ensures you're doing what's right for both the individual and the organization, fostering growth and alignment for everyone involved.

# Change the People or Change the People

### By Tania Bengtsson

When I begin working with a client, we first get the right structure, then make sure our leadership team is full of rock stars, and continue to build our bench at every level of the company the same way.

This process helps the company and every member of the team gain clarity on accountabilities and get better execution. It also uncovers issues that need to be solved.

To achieve its vision, a company must effectively solve its issues. And the core root cause of the issues is people, making *people* and *results* the same. Ultimately, when we encounter people issues, we need to "Change the people or change the people."

**The first "change the people" is developing your existing team:**

1. **Fully Embrace Your Vision at Every Level:** simply bringing clarity to roles, expectations, and using the tools available brings momentum and better execution.

2. **Implement Leadership & Management Training**: Anyone who leads and manages people has that as their #1 most critical role because nothing is more important. Shockingly, 86% of leaders & managers are accidental. A common, yet flawed, approach is thinking someone who is great at a job will make a great leader for people doing that job. It's rarely the case. Just like you provided them with training when they were onboarded, you must now provide leadership training, programs, plans, and mentorship to develop their skills.

3. **Sabbatical Management Mindset**: Leaders who train, mentor, delegate, and empower their people to make decisions effectively create extensions of themselves by allowing their people to operate autonomously. Otherwise, leaders become bottlenecks and burned out. Leaders need space to become what their growing company needs, capacity for strategic thinking, and most importantly time to develop and coach their people.

This approach requires time, effort, and a mindset shift. When stress is high, people commonly revert to their comfort zones, which is doing the work themselves. Effective leaders must resist this urge to rescue their people and instead focus on coaching and developing their team members.

After sincere efforts to develop your existing team, there will be some who can't, or won't, adapt. That's when we move to the second "change the people":

1. **Reassign Them To The Right Seat**: Love your people enough to put them in seats where they can be successful and the company wins too. Leaving someone in the wrong seat creates the wrong people. That is a recipe for turnover of high performers, lack of execution, and lower profit.
2. **Removal**: In cases of wrong people (cultural misalignment), wrong seat (persistent underperformance), or if you don't have a seat to reassign them to, the kindest action is to set them free to find opportunities elsewhere. There's a company out there with a better cultural fit and/or seat for them to thrive. It's a win-win.

The concept is simple, but execution is often challenging. We confuse caring about people with hurting their feelings. The reality is, we're hurting them more by allowing the situation to continue.

Leaders must be kind, loving, strong, and brave. Great leaders lead with these attributes, not fear. Fear often creeps in when change is necessary because change can be scary. Leaders must model the change they want to see. This authenticity and commitment to growth is what makes a leader worth following.

Whether it's developing your team or making tough people decisions, to achieve your vision you must be prepared to "change the people or change the people."

# Connecting Human Energy
## oneness

### By Kevin Hundal

In organizational leadership, embracing **oneness** can transform a good business into a great one. This concept emphasizes unity and purpose throughout an organization.

Oneness is about connecting human energy to **elevate, empower,** and **enrich** everyone and everything around us.

This manifests as the journey towards becoming the best team possible, embodying "one vision, one voice, and one team approach."

Oneness involves everyone in the organization, leveraging the innate energy within us all. When human connections are strong across all levels of the accountability chart, it elevates the entire company, providing a competitive advantage in the marketplace.

To bring this oneness paradigm to life, I've developed the **1-3-1 Framework**—a simple, yet powerful, approach that empowers everyone within the organization to contribute more effectively.

Have you ever been approached by a colleague or direct report and left the conversation feeling overwhelmed or lost? Do you wish there was a way to make these interactions more productive and less draining?

If you're anything like me, you look for opportunities to coach and develop the people around you, ultimately enriching them and the entire organization.

Here's how the 1-3-1 Framework comes to life: Before bringing an issue to someone else in the organization, set aside 15 minutes to work through the following steps.

1. **One Root Cause:** When identifying an issue, determine the root cause. For example, if deadlines are consistently missed, is the root cause unclear expectations or resource constraints? Pinpointing the core problem prevents conversations from veering into multiple, unrelated issues.

2. **Three Potential Solutions**: Once the root cause is identified, challenge yourself to develop three potential solutions. This

process pushes you beyond the obvious answer and often leads to more innovative solutions.

3. **One Strong Recommendation**: Finally, choose the solution you're willing to stand behind confidently. Ask yourself, "What am I ready to put my name behind?"

**By embracing this 1-3-1 framework, organizations can:**

- Encourage stakeholder buy-in
- Reduce issue handoffs (eliminating the "monkey on the back" syndrome)
- Develop problem-solving skills at all levels
- Create personal development opportunities
- Foster a culture of oneness throughout the organization

Implementing the 1-3-1 framework creates a common language within the organization. Imagine the power of 70 teammates practicing 1-3-1 every day in the organization. The impact multiplies creating exponential growth for not only the organization but also the individual contributors.

This approach also challenges leaders to look inward, breaking down personal ego and promoting self-reflection. By embracing oneness and the 1-3-1 Framework, you can transform your organization into a unified, high-performing team that proactively solves issues and takes advantage of opportunities.

Take a few minutes to locate where your organization is today:

On a scale of 1-10, how strong is the connection across all of the teams: _____

What 3 actions can increase your score by 10% this week:

1. _____
2. _____
3. _____

Start connecting human energy within your organization today. Embrace the 1-3-1 Framework and witness the transformation as your teams elevate, empower, and enrich one another towards bringing your vision to reality.

# Win the Week

### By Dan Wallace

In sessions I ask leadership teams to set objectives in progressively shorter increments of time, with increasing detail as the time frame grows shorter. We work from 10-years to 3-years to 1-year, and finally, to the quarterly plan. Achieving these objectives looks like this:

- To win your 10-year, you have to win your 3-year 3 times.
- To win your 3-year, you have to win your 1-year 3 times.
- To win your 1-year, you have to win 4 consecutive quarters.

So how do you win a quarter? By winning 13 weeks in a row.

The week is the actual increment of time in which we do work and hold ourselves accountable. Achieving your biggest, most important long-term objectives comes down to your ability to consistently win week after week.

So how do you win a week? By doing 4 things:

1. Hit your weekly numbers - the metrics that ensure you are executing your existing business well.
2. Keep your quarterly projects - the initiatives through which you are building your future business - on track.
3. Get your team-based to-do items - short-term commitments between team members - done.
4. Solve the issues that came up during the week that are getting in the way.

As long as the strategy and plan are sound, if you focus relentlessly on those four things, and you get them done consistently, you'll win.

Made in the USA
Middletown, DE
03 February 2025

69995355R00024